TIME-LIFE
Early Learning Program

The Great A B C Treasure Hunt

TIME LIFE for Children ™

ALEXANDRIA, VIRGINIA

Here come my friends Amy and Zachary, the alphabet mice! Join us in a fantastic treasure hunt as we search for hidden letters in Alphabet Land!

Note to Parents

From teaching letter recognition to building vocabulary, *The Great ABC Treasure Hunt* can help your child take several first steps toward reading. The book contains 26 poems, each devoted to one letter of the alphabet. As you read the poems aloud, your child will enjoy listening to the cadence and alliteration of the words. Such readings will also introduce—and eventually reinforce—the sound of each letter.

Several questions appear with each poem. The questions direct your child to identify an activity being performed by Amy and Zachary, the twin alphabet mice, or to scan the art for animals and objects beginning with the featured letter. As a way of exposing your child to new vocabulary, almost every item in each illustration starts with that letter.

The Great ABC Treasure Hunt can also help your child learn the shapes of letters. Hidden in the illustration for each letter are 10 uppercase and 10 lowercase examples of that letter. Some letters are especially challenging to spot; the key at the end of the book tells where to find each one.

Once your child has learned to recognize and sound out letters, encourage him or her to look for them elsewhere—in road signs, at the grocery store, on the pages of newspapers and magazines. As well as being fun, this pursuit can lead your child to real treasure—the ability to read on one's own.

TREASURE

Aa

An alligator's eating
All the **A**'s that he can spot.
He's munched the **a** in **a**corn,
The **a** in **a**pricot.

He's gobbled **a**'s in **a**ba**c**us,
And one in **a**pple tree;
Soon he will have eaten
All the **A**'s that he can see!

An armadillo artist
And an acrobat or two,
An astronaut, an antelope,
All say it's up to you:

"Find 10 big **A**'s
And 10 small **a**'s.
When you've spied each one,
You'll save the day for letter **A**—
Come on, let's join the fun!"

What are Amy and Zachary
riding in?
What is the aardvark
driving?

Bb

Let's celebrate the letter **B**.
Count all the **B** words you can see:
There's beach and bucket, broom and ball—
Keep looking and you'll find them all!

A bear in bed with bugle bright
Toots birthday tunes with all her might.
While down below, a billy goat
Plays bagpipes in a bathtub boat!

A beaver who comes floating by
Reads ballads to a butterfly.
Now look around for baby bear;
He's blowing bubbles in the air!

Binoculars, a hat that's tied,
And something all bears love to ride;
Balloons and bottles, bees and birds—
Oh, **B**! You start so many words!

*What's the bear with
the bucket doing?*

*How many bananas are
in the brown bag?*

Cc

To find Carol's caramel-colored cat,
follow the paw prints in the picture.
What is the cockatoo doing?
That cheetah's leg looks broken—
what is it using to walk?
Did you notice that the big
and little **c** are shaped alike?

My caramel-colored cat is lost.
Oh, won't you help me, please?
I'm sure that we can find her
Among the big and little **C**'s.

The cuckoo in the clock believes
She's chatting with a calf.
A chimp who uses chopsticks
Says he thought he heard her laugh.

A camel with a compass
Says she's headed way out west.
A cricket playing cello
Says, "Check the treasure chest."

A cook with corn and celery,
A clown with curly hair,
Say "Look at all the **C** words—
You're bound to find her there!"

Dd

Down in the dell
Where the dandelion grows,
A dragonfly danced
On a dinosaur's toes.
The dodos in the daisies
Played with dominoes,
While the Duke and the Duchess
Did their do-si-dos!

*Can you find the 10 big **D**'s
and 10 little **d**'s hidden
in this picture?*

Eggs have one
And **ee**ls have two.
There's one in m**e**,
But none in you.

Thr**ee** has two
And so does s**eve**n.
How many are there
In **ele**ve**n?

Guess who is about to enter the school?
How many engines can you count?
Can you find the "Exit" sign?
Who is exercising outside the school?

Ff

Fe, Fi, Fo,
Fiddly–i–o,
Five friendly fairies fly to and fro.
But they've flown too far
And they don't know where they are
And they have to be home before Friday!

Fe, Fi, Fo,
Fiddly–i–a,
A fine flashing firefly can show them the way.
With her flickering light,
She'll make everything bright—
And they'll all be back home before Friday!

Count the frogs on the Ferris wheel.
What do you think Amy is about to catch?

Friday
15

Gg

Someone grabbed the gumdrops
From the gumdrop tree.
They'd been growing there forever;
Now they're gone, as you can see.

The gray goose gathering garlic
In the garden just might be
The one who grabbed the gumdrops
From the gumdrop tree.

"Not me! Couldn't be!"
Said the gray goose with a glare.
"I was home with the gander.
Ask the grizzly bear!"

But the grizzly guzzled honey
And attempted to look gruff.
"Go and ask that goofy giraffe—
He's surely tall enough!"

Giraffe, with a laugh,
Giggled, "No, not me!
I'd never grab the gumdrops
From the gumdrop tree."

Gaze at every **G** word
And soon you will see
Just who grabbed the gumdrops
From the gumdrop tree.

Who is wearing galoshes?
Can you find the groundhog
  pointing at the globe?
*Don't forget to find all the hidden **G**'s!*

Hh

Hey, Hidey, Ho,
See the hippo tiptoe,
See the hound dog hiding in a hollow tree.
There's a hare in the air; how *did* it get up there?
And a hummingbird is humming to a honeybee.

Hide-and-seek is the name of this game;
Where's the hamster? Who's in the hay?
Up hill, down hill, hunt through the town 'til
You find all the **H** words along the way!

What are Amy and Zachary doing?
Who is hiding behind the hydrant?

Ii

My islands are both far away
And very close it seems,
In my imagination,
And sometimes in my dreams.

My islands are invisible
To everyone but me.
I think—I blink—I close my eyes,
And I'm there instantly!

Find an island shaped like a big I;
  find one shaped like a small i.
Can you find the iguana eating an ice-cream cone?

At a quarter to six
On the jumping-jack clock,
The jitterbugs cry,
"Everybody, let's rock!"

So the jaguar plays jive
And the jackals play jazz
While the jellyfish drums out
Razz-a-ma-tazz.

Who is jogging through the jam session?

Jj

Kk

The King was reading the alphabet.
When he came to **K**, he began to fret.
On the page before him, printed in plain view
Were the words, "**K** is for Kinkajou."

The *kinkajou* is a furry mammal that lives in the forests of Mexico and South America. It can hang by its tail from the branch of a tree.

So the King consulted his wise old knight,
Who fell to his knees and began to recite
All of the **K** words that he ever knew,
Like kettle, and ketchup, and kangaroo . . .

*Look in all five pictures to find a total of 10 big **K**'s and 10 little **k**'s. What is Zachary doing?*

"**K** is for King," he cried in dismay.
"And what *is* a kinkajou, anyway?"
Then his face turned pink and red and blue
As he contemplated the kinkajou.

He rushed to the kitchen to ask the Queen
If a kinkajou was anything she'd ever seen.
"Not I!" she said with a wink or two.
"No, I've never laid eyes on a kinkajou!"

Kaleidoscope, kite, koala, kazoo,
Kitten and keyhole, and Kalamazoo;
Kiwi and kerchief, and kitchen sink too.
But he never once mentioned a kinkajou!

Returning to the shade of his kumquat tree,
The King saw a kinkajou, kind as could be.
Right then and there, he changed his view:
"**K** is for King," he said, "*and* for kinkajou!"

L l

The lullaby lady is singing her song,
And you will be sleeping before very long.
You'd like to stay up, and although you may try,
There's just no resisting her lullaby.

She sings about lanterns that light up the night,
Lizards on ladders, and lambs snowy white.

She sings about lavender lions who leap,
Oh, the lullaby lady will lull you to sleep.

She sings about leopards, and larks on the wing,
Pajamas on llamas, and lilacs in spring,

And loons who are laughing on lakes that are deep;
Oh, the lullaby lady will lull you to sleep.

What is the lamb licking?
Who is lacing the shoe?
What are Amy and Zachary selling?

Mm

Monkey found a mirror bright.
"What's this?" he said in sudden fright.
"I think a monster is in there
With many teeth and too much hair!"

Can you find the mole's mailbox?
What is Amy teaching Zachary?
Don't forget to look in all four pictures
*to find the hidden **M**'s!*

A madcap mule then came along,
And said, "I think you two are wrong.
I see only a silly face
Locked inside that glassy place."

Then came a mole from underground
To look into the mirror round.
"Oh my!" said Mole, "His head is flat.
I'm glad I do not look like that!"

Anytime and anywhere
A mirror only shows what's there.
It's your turn now—whom can it be
That mule and mole and monkey see?

Nn

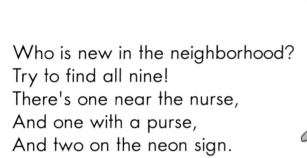

Who is new in the neighborhood?
Try to find all nine!
There's one near the nurse,
And one with a purse,
And two on the neon sign.

Next to the newts in navy blue suits,
Are two more hammering nails.
There's one in the nest—
But where are the rest?
Find two more nightingales.

*Where are the last
two nightingales?
What are Amy and
Zachary delivering?*

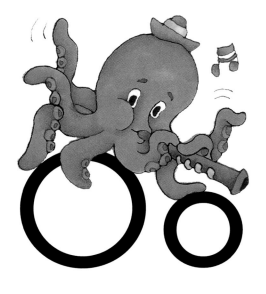

Once there was an off-key owl
Who couldn't hoot quite right.
He went "Oompah! Oompah! Olé!"
And it echoed through the night.

What color is the orangutan's hair?
What has eight legs and plays
   an oboe?
What other animals do you
   see whose names begin
   with the letter O?

One night the wisest of the owls
Flew out of the old oak tree.
And asked that he be taught to sing
This offbeat melody.

The animals objected
And they left him on his own
To go "Oompah! Oompah! Olé!"
In an orange tree alone.

The moral: It's not wrong to sing
A different kind of song.
Now the forest rings with "Oompah! Olé's!"
All the loud night long.

P p

I've got my shopping list with me;
I'm going to the store.
But all it says is the letter **P**—
What could that stand for?

Pineapple? Pizza? Paper plates?
Potatoes? Or a pear?
Pillows? Pickles? Purple skates?
Or party hats to wear?

A pair of patent leather shoes?
A present that is tied?
With so many **P** words,
Who can choose?
Oh! Why don't YOU decide?

*Pick your favorite **P** word.*
Is it in the picture?

Here's a question just for you:
Which letter always follows **Q**?

Look at **q**ueen
      and **q**uack
            and **q**uite.
Have you got the rule **q**uite right?

Look at **q**uarter,
   quail,
         and **q**uiz.
Can you guess what the letter is?

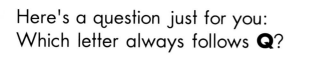

In every word, the letter **Q**
Is always followed by a U.

What sound does a duck make?
What time does the clock say?

Rr

I'm a ribbon in the sky, but don't wear me in your hair;
I'm harder to hold than a mouthful of air.
I come out only when there's rain and then sun;
My colors shine bright when the bad weather's done.

What am I?

I am always running and tripping over rocks.
But I never win a race—I have no shoes or socks.
I am always in my bed, but never do I sleep.
I ramble on my rolling way to join the ocean deep.

What am I?

Can you help the robin reach her nest?
What sort of racket game do you think
 the rat is about to play?
What are Zachary and
 Amy doing?
Did you find the 10 big **R**'s
 and the 10 small **r**'s?

Ss

Sheep wear wool and snails sport shells.
Squids squirt ink and skunks spray smells.
Seagulls soar and spiders spin.
Stags grow antlers; snakes shed skin.

Stoats change coats to white from brown.
Sloths spend lifetimes upside down.
Sparrows sing and scorpions sting.
Each one does a special thing!

What sort of diving are Zachary and Amy doing?
Did you find the swordfish? What about the sunflowers?
Can you find the stoat wearing the coat?

T for two and two for tea;
Two is always company.

Tick-tack-toe is played by two—
So many things can two friends do.

TUESDAY TANGO

Two can tango, two can race;
Two for tag, 'cause two can chase.

Two could never be a crowd.
Two can talk and laugh out loud.

Two can play a game of catch.
Two can be a perfect match.

Two can talk by telephone—
Two are never all alone.

Two can tote and two can tug.
Two take turns; two can hug.

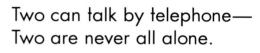

Two suits us right to a tee,
For two can be just you and me!

What game are Amy and Zachary playing?
See how many toucans you can find!
What is Amy sitting on?
Where is the turtle with the telescope?

Uu

Upon my head a cresty crown
Of feathers growing upside down;
Hanging down beneath my grin
Grow feathers on a flap of skin.

Through rainy forests I can fly
And always keep myself quite dry.
I love to sing—have you heard?
I am a real umbrella bird!

*What are Amy and Zachary wearing as they
    strum their ukuleles?*
What do you call a bicycle with one wheel?
*Can you uncover all the **U**'s in the jungle?*

The umbrella bird lives in forests of Mexico
and South America. This unusual creature is
distinguished by its crest, which resembles
an umbrella.

Vv

One day the vulture had a guest.
He dressed up in his velvet vest.
(His visitor was quite impressed.)
And when the sun sank in the west,
The vulture served what they loved best:
Vegetables!

Here are some names that start with V:
Vincent, Victor, Van, Vito, and Virgil.
What would you name the
vulture and the Viking?

HOME SWEET HOME

The wiggle-waggle worm went out
To see the world one day.
He waved good-bye and
Wiggle-waggled on his winding way.

*What did the wiggle-waggle worm
see that starts with the letter **W**?
What are Amy and Zachary doing?*

He saw where whales and wild wolves sleep,
And why the weeping willows weep.

As he wandered with the winds,
A wealth of wonders did he see:
A woodchuck who was chucking wood;
A wishing well; a wallaby.

And when he wiggle-waggled home,
A wiser worm was he!

Xx

When treasure has been hidden,
It's **X** that marks the spot.
But it is not the **X**'s job
To start out words a lot.

An **x** exists in mi**x**ing,
And one appears in fo**x**.
One's mixed in with fi**x**ing,
And one ends cardboard bo**x**.

Three **X**'s mean three kisses
When written as a sign.
There's even an **x**
In Tyrannosaurus Re**x**;
Oh, **X**! You're one of a kind!

*Only a few words start with the letter **X**.
Can you find an x-ray, two xylophones,
and the king named Xerxes?*

Yy

The yaks sailed off on their yellow yacht
With yogurt and yo-yos—they took a lot!
What else did they pack for their year-long trip?
Yams and yarn and yummy dip—
And lots of yakaroni!

*Find 10 big **Y**'s and 10 little **y**'s.*
What is the yellow part of an egg called?
How can you tell that one yak is sleepy?

Z is for **z**ebra, **Z** is for **z**oo;
Z is for **z**ig**z**ag, and **z**ucchini too.

Zither and **z**esty are on the **Z** list;
There's **z**ipper and **z**eppelin—but I'm always missed!

Zenith and **z**innia, **z**ero and **z**one:
These are all **Z** words, but I am unknown.
And that's why I've asked for a page of my own!

I'm a **z**ebu—
And **Z** is for me too!

A *zebu* is an ox–like animal that lives in many Asian countries.

What instrument is Amy playing?
Can you trace the zigzag walkway
*   with your finger?*

From A to Z and in between,
You know what all the letters mean!
And that's what you've been looking for.
A treasure now and evermore:
The ALPHABET!

Amy and Zachary's Alphabet Key

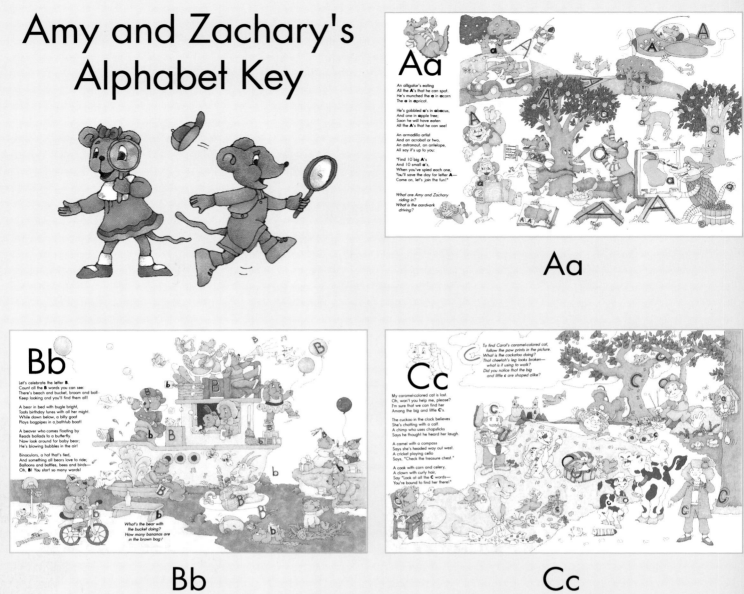

Aa

Bb

Cc

Dd

Ee

Ff

Fe, Fi, Fo,
Fiddly-i—o.
Five friendly fairies fly to and fro.
But they've flown too far
And they don't know where they are
And they have to be home before Friday!

Fe, Fi, Fo,
Fiddly-i—o,
A fine flashing firefly can show them the way.
With her flickering light,
She'll make everything bright—
And they'll all be back home before Friday!

*Count the frogs on the Ferris wheel.
What do you think Amy is about to catch?*

Ff

Gg

Someone grabbed the gumdrops
From the gumdrop tree.
They'd been growing there forever;
Now they're gone, as you can see.

The gray goose gathering garlic
In the garden just might be
The one who grabbed the gumdrops
From the gumdrop tree.

"Not me! Couldn't be!"
Said the gray goose with a glare,
"I was home with the gander.
Ask the grizzly bear!"

But the grizzly guzzled honey
And attempted to look gruff.
"Go and ask that goofy giraffe—
He's surely tall enough!"

Giraffe, with a laugh,
Giggled, "No, not me!
I'd never grab the gumdrops
From the gumdrop tree."

Gaze at every **G** word
And soon you will see
Just who grabbed the gumdrops
From the gumdrop tree.

*Who is wearing galoshes?
Can you find the groundhog
pointing at the globe?
Don't forget to find all the hidden **G**'s!*

Gg

Hh

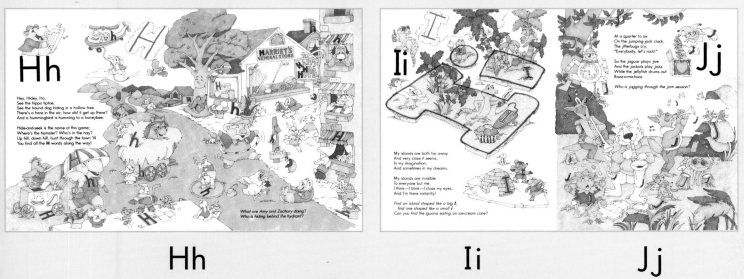

Hey, Hidey, Ho,
See the hippo tiptoe,
See the hound dog hiding in a hollow tree.
There's a hare in the air; how did it get up there?
And a hummingbird is humming to a honeybee.

Hide-and-seek is the name of this game;
Where's the hamster? Who's in the hay?
Up hill, down hill, hunt through the town 'til
You find all the **H** words along the way!

*What are Amy and Zachary doing?
Who is hiding behind the hydrant?*

Hh

Ii

My islands are both far away
And very close it seems,
In my imagination,
And sometimes in my dreams.

My islands are invisible
To everyone but me.
I think—I blink—I close my eyes,
And I'm there instantly!

*Find an island shaped like a big **I**;
find one shaped like a small **I**.
Can you find the iguana eating an ice-cream cone?*

Ii

Jj

At a quarter to six
On the jumping-jack clock,
The jitterbugs cry,
"Everybody, let's rock!"

So the jaguar plays jive
And the jackals play jazz
While the jellyfish drums out
Razz-a-ma-tazz.

Who is jogging through the jam session?

Jj

Kk

The King was reading the alphabet.
When he came to **K**, he began to fret.
On the page before him, printed in plain view
Were the words, "**K** is for Kinkajou."

"**K** is for King," he cried in dismay.
"And what is a kinkajou, anyway?"
Then his face turned pink and red and blue
As he contemplated the kinkajou.

He rushed to the kitchen to ask the Queen
If a kinkajou was anything she'd ever seen.
"No! I!" she said with a wink or two.
"No, I've never laid eyes on a kinkajou!"

So the King consulted his wise old knight,
Who fell to his knees and began to recite
All of the **K** words that he ever knew,
Like kettle, and ketchup, and kangaroo . . .

Kaleidoscope, kite, koala, kazoo,
Kitten and keyhole, and Kalamazoo,
Kiwi and kerchief, and kitchen sink too.
But he never once mentioned a kinkajou!

Returning to the shade of his kumquat tree,
The King saw a kinkajou, kind as could be.
Right then and there, he changed his view:
"**K** is for King," he said, "and for kinkajou!"

The kinkajou is a furry mammal that lives in the forests of Mexico and South America. It can hang by its tail from the branch of a tree.

*Look in all five pictures to find a total of 10 big **K**'s and 10 little **k**'s.
What is Zachary doing?*

Kk

Ll

The lullaby lady is singing her song,
And you will be sleeping before very long.
You'd like to stay up, and although you may try,
There's just no resisting her lullaby.

She sings about lanterns that light up the night,
Lizards on ladders, and lambs snowy white.

She sings about leopards, and larks on the wing,
Pajamas on llamas, and lilacs in spring,

She sings about lavender lions who leap;
Oh, the lullaby lady will lull you to sleep.

And loons who are laughing on lakes that are deep;
Oh, the lullaby lady will lull you to sleep.

*What is the lamb licking?
Who is lacing the shoe?
What are Amy and Zachary selling?*

Ll

Mm

Monkey found a mirror bright.
"What's this?" he said in sudden fright.
"I think a monster is in there
With many teeth and too much hair!"

Then came a mole from underground
To look into the mirror round.
"Oh my!" said Mole, "His head is flat.
I'm glad I do not look like that!"

A madcap mule then came along,
And said, "I think you two are wrong.
I see only a silly face
Locked inside that glassy place."

Anytime and anywhere
A mirror only shows what's there.
It's your turn now—whom can it be
That mule and mole and monkey see?

Can you find the mole's mailbox?
What is Amy teaching Zachary?
Don't forget to look in all four pictures
to find the hidden M's!

Nn

Who is new in the neighborhood?
Try to find all nine!
There's one near the nurse,
And one with a purse,
And two on the neon sign.

Next to the newts in navy blue suits,
Are two more hammering nails.
There's one in the nest—
But where are the rest?
Find two more nightingales.

Where are the last
two nightingales?
What are Amy and
Zachary delivering?

Mm

Nn

Oo

Once there was an off-key owl
Who couldn't hoot quite right.
He went "Oompah! Oompah! Olé!"
And it echoed through the night.

The animals objected
And they left him on his own
To go "Oompah! Oompah! Olé!"
In an orange tree alone.

One night the wisest of the owls
Flew out of the old oak tree.
And asked that he be taught to sing
This offbeat melody.

The moral: It's not wrong to sing
A different kind of song.
Now the forest rings with "Oompah! Olé's!"
All the loud night long.

What color is the orangutan's hair?
What has eight legs and plays
an oboe?
What other animals do you
see whose names begin
with the letter O?

Pp

I've got my shopping list with me,
I'm going to the store.
But all it says is the letter P—
What could that stand for?

Pineapple? Pizza? Paper plates?
Potatoes? Or a pear?
Pillows? Pickles? Purple skates?
Or party hats to wear?

A pair of patent leather shoes?
A present that is tied?
With so many P words,
Who can choose?
Oh! Why don't YOU decide?

Pick your favorite P word.
Is it in the picture?

Qq

Here's a question just for you:
Which letter always follows Q?
Look at queen
and quack
and quite.
Have you got the rule quite right?

Look at quarter,
quail,
and quiz.
Can you guess what the letter is?

In every word, the letter Q
Is always followed by a U.

What sound does a duck make?
What time does the clock say?

Oo

Pp

Qq

Rr

I'm a ribbon in the sky, but don't wear me in your hair,
I'm harder to hold than a mouthful of air;
I come out only when there's rain and then sun;
My colors shine bright when the bad weather's done.
What am I?

I am always running and tripping over rocks.
But I never win a race—I have no shoes or socks.
I am always in my bed, but never do I sleep.
I ramble on my rolling way to join the ocean deep.
What am I?

Can you help the robin reach her nest?
What sort of racket game do you think
the rat is about to play?
What are Zachary and
Amy doing?
Did you find the 10 big R's
and the 10 small r's?

Ss

Sheep wear wool and snails sport shells.
Squids squirt ink and skunks spray smells.
Seagulls soar and spiders spin.
Stags grow antlers; snakes shed skin.
Stoats change coats to white from brown.
Sloths spend lifetimes upside down.
Sparrows sing and scorpions sting.
Each one does a special thing!

What sort of diving are Zachary and Amy doing?
Did you find the swordfish? What about the sunflowers?
Can you find the stoat wearing the coat?

Rr

Ss

Tt

T for two and two for tea;
Two is always company.

Two can play a game of catch.
Two can be a perfect match.

Two can talk by telephone—
Two are never all alone.

Tick-tack-toe is played by two—
So many things can two friends do.

Two can tango, two can race;
Two for tag, 'cause two can chase.

Two can tote and two can tug.
Two take turns; two can hug.

Two suits us right to a tee,
For two can be just you and me!

Two could never be a crowd.
Two can talk and laugh out loud.

What game are Amy and Zachary playing?
See how many toucans you can find!
What is Amy sitting on?
Where is the turtle with the telescope?

Uu

Upon my head a cresty crown
Of feathers growing upside down;
Hanging down beneath my grin
Grow feathers on a flap of skin.

Through rainy forests I can fly
And always keep myself quite dry.
I love to sing—have you heard?
I am a real umbrella bird!

What are Amy and Zachary wearing as they
strum their ukuleles?
What do you call a bicycle with one wheel?
Can you uncover all the U's in the jungle?

The umbrella bird lives in forests of Mexico
and South America. This unusual creature is
distinguished by its crest, which resembles
an umbrella.

Vv

One day the vulture had a guest.
He dressed up in his velvet vest.
(His visitor was quite impressed.)
And when the sun sank in the west,
The vulture served what they loved best:
Vegetables!

Here are some names that start with V:
Vincent, Victor, Van, Vita, and Virgil.
What would you name the
vulture and the Viking?

HOME SWEET HOME

Ww

The wiggle-waggle worm went out
To see the world one day.
He waved good-bye and
Wiggle-waggled on his winding way.

As he wandered with the winds,
A wealth of wonders did he see:
A woodchuck who was chucking wood;
A wishing well; a wallaby.

What did the wiggle-waggle worm
see that starts with the letter W?
What are Amy and Zachary doing?

He saw where whales and wild wolves sleep,
And why the weeping willows weep.

And when he wiggle-waggled home,
A wiser worm was he!

Xx

When treasure has been hidden,
It's X that marks the spot.
But it is not the X's job
To start out words a lot.

An x exists in mixing,
And one appears in fox.
One's mixed in with faxing,
And one ends cardboard box.

Three X's mean three kisses
When written as a sign.
There's even an x
In Tyrannosaurus Rex;
Oh, X! You're one of a kind!

I ♥ YOU
XXX

Only a few words start with the letter X.
Can you find an x-ray, two xylophones,
and the king named Xerxes?

Yy

The yaks sailed off on their yellow yacht
With yogurt and yoyos—they took a lot!
What else did they pack for their year-long trip?
Yams and yarn and yummy dip—
And lots of yakaroni!

Find 10 big Y's and 10 little y's.
What is the yellow part of an egg called?
How can you tell that one yak is sleepy?

What instrument is Amy playing?
Can you trace the zigzag walkway
with your finger?

Zz

Z is for zebra, Z is for zoo;
Z is for zigzag, and zucchini too.

Zither and zesty are on the Z list;
There's zipper and zeppelin—but I'm always missed!

Zenith and zinnia, zero and zone:
These are all Z words, but I am unknown.

And that's why I've asked for a page of my own!

I'm a Zebu—
And Z is for me too!

A zebu is an ox-like
animal that lives in
many Asian countries.

TIME-LIFE for CHILDREN™

Publisher: Robert H. Smith
Managing Editor: Neil Kagan
Editorial Directors: Jean Burke Crawford,
  Patricia Daniels, Allan Fallow, Karin Kinney
Editorial Coordinator: Elizabeth Ward
Product Managers: Cassandra P. Ford,
  Margaret Mooney
Assistant Product Manager: Shelley L. Schimkus
Production Manager: Prudence G. Harris
Administrative Assistant: Rebecca C. Christoffersen
Editorial Consultant: Sara Mark
Special Contributor: Jacqueline A. Ball

Produced by Joshua Morris Publishing, Inc.
Wilton, Connecticut 06897.
Series Director: Michael J. Morris
Creative Director: William N. Derraugh
Illustrator: Pat Hoggan
Author: Muff Singer
Design Consultant: Francis G. Morgan
Designers: Jamie Cain, Nora Voutas

CONSULTANTS
Dr. Lewis P. Lipsitt, an internationally recognized specialist on childhood development, was the 1990 recipient of the Nicholas Hobbs Award for science in the service of children. He serves as science director for the American Psychological Association and is a professor of psychology and medical science at Brown University, where he is director of the Child Study Center.

Dr. Judith A. Schickedanz, an authority on the education of preschool children, is an associate professor of early childhood education at the Boston University School of Education, where she also directs the Early Childhood Learning Laboratory. Her published work includes *More Than the ABC's: Early Stages of Reading and Writing Development* as well as several textbooks and many scholarly papers. Dr. Schickedanz has served on the Early Childhood Committee of the International Reading Association and has been a consultant to the Children's Television Workshop, producers of *Sesame Street.*

First printing. Printed in Hong Kong.
Published simultaneously in Canada.

Time Life Inc. is a wholly owned subsidiary of THE TIME INC, BOOK COMPANY.

TIME-LIFE is a trademark of Time Warner Inc. U.S.A.

Time Life Inc. offers a wide range of fine publications, including home video products. For subscription information, call 1-800-621-7026, or write TIME-LIFE BOOKS, P.O. Box C-32068, Richmond, Virginia 23261-2068.

Library of Congress Cataloging-in-Publication Data
The Great ABC Treasure Hunt

     p. cm. – (Time-Life early learning program)
    Summary: An illustrated collection of twenty-six poems featuring objects, animals, and activities for each letter of the alphabet. Hidden letters within the illustrations increase letter recognition.

    ISBN 0-8094-9254-7 (trade). – ISBN 0-8094-9255-5 (lib. bdg.)

    1. English language-Alphabet-Juvenile literature. 2. Alphabet Rhymes.
[1. Alphabet] I .Time-Life for Children (Firm) II. Series.PE1155.G74 1991
421:1–dc20
[E]   90-11152
                                             CIP
                                             AC